Magnets

By Julie Haydon

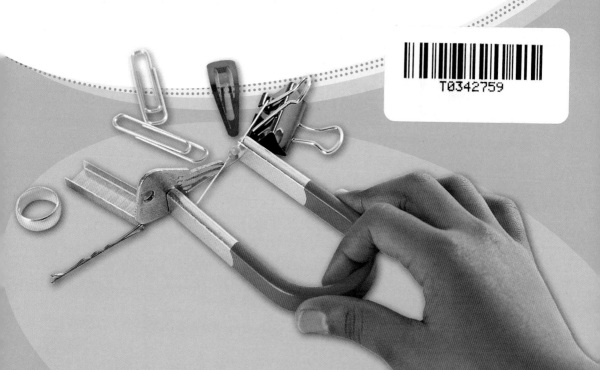

Contents

How a Magnet Attracts Objects

A magnet is an object that can pull, or attract, some metal objects towards it.

A magnet is usually made of iron or steel.

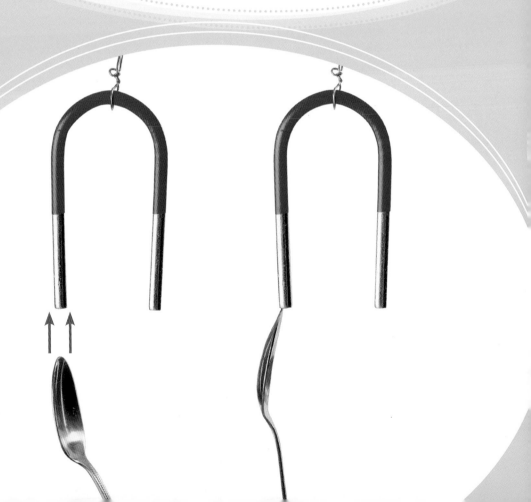

A magnet attracts objects by a special force, called magnetism.

There is an area of magnetism around every magnet. This area is called a magnetic field. A magnet can only attract an object that is inside its magnetic field.

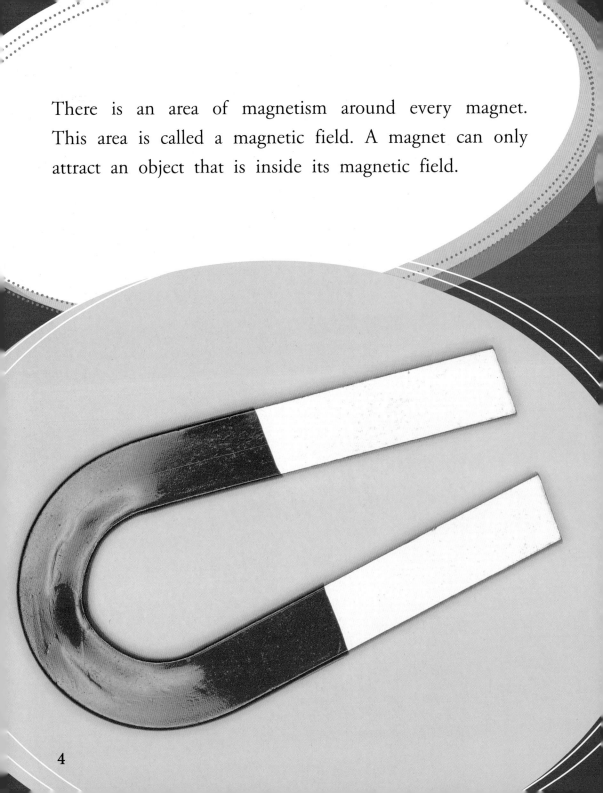

Magnetic fields are invisible. When tiny pieces of iron are attracted to a magnet, the shape of its magnetic field becomes visible.

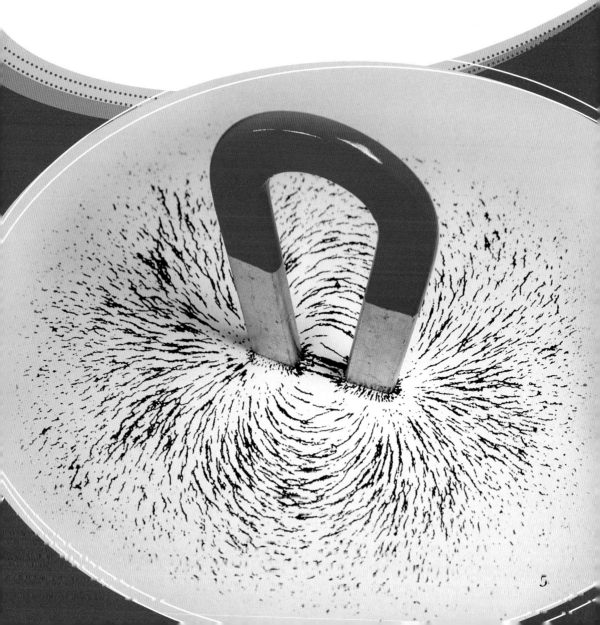

Objects that are attracted to a magnet are called magnetic objects. Iron or steel objects are magnetic.

Objects that are not attracted to a magnet are called non-magnetic objects. Rubber, wooden and plastic objects are non-magnetic.

A magnet has two poles. The south pole is at one end of the magnet and the north pole is at the other end.

The same poles of two magnets push away from each other.

The south pole of a magnet attracts the north pole of another magnet.

Magnets attract objects by the force of magnetism.

north pole   south pole

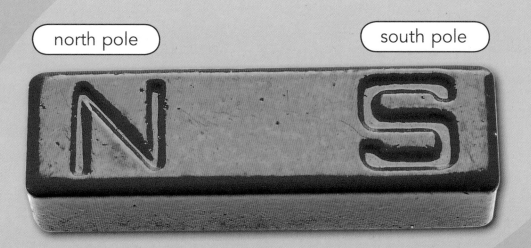

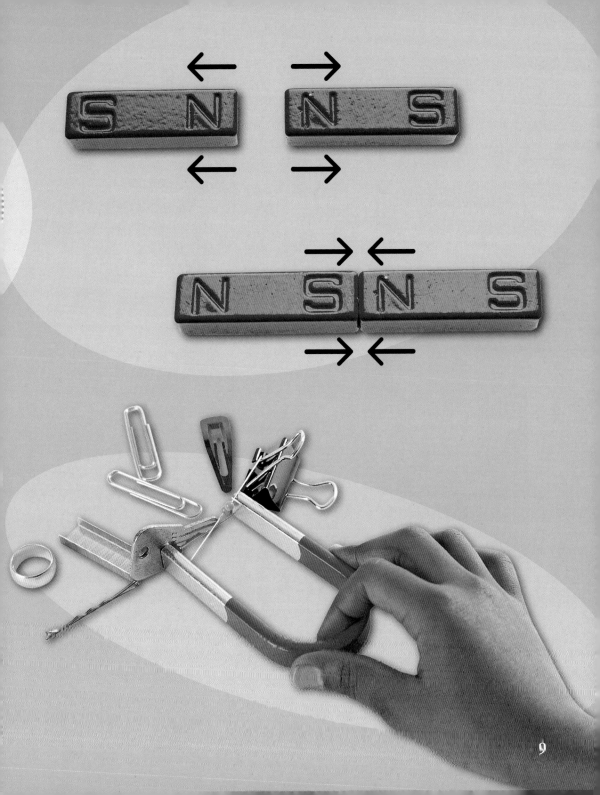

An Experiment with Magnets

Goal

To prove that a magnet will attract objects made of iron or steel.

Materials

You will need:

- a magnet

- a box containing rubber bands, toothpicks, marbles, paper clips, nails, pins, hair pins, staples, scissors, buttons

- an A4 sheet of paper

- a pen

- a ruler

- an empty jar.

Steps

1. Rule a line through the middle of the sheet of paper.

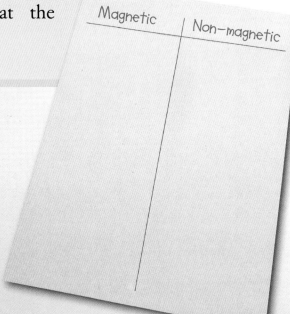

2. Write the heading 'Magnetic' at the top of one column and the heading 'Non-magnetic' at the top of the other column.

3. Hold the magnet over each group
   of objects in turn.

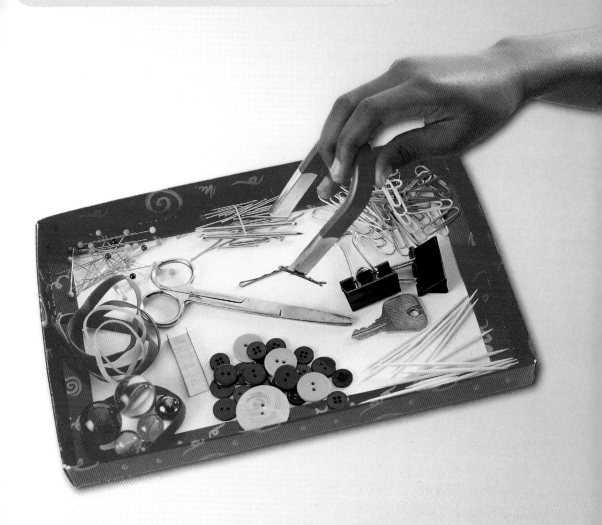

4. Place the objects that the magnet picks up in the jar.

5. Write the names of the objects the magnet picks up under the heading 'Magnetic'.

Magnetic	Non-magnetic
pins	
nails	
paper clips	
hair pins	
staples	
scissors	

6. Leave the objects that the magnet does not pick up in the box.

7. Write the names of the objects that the magnet does not pick up under the heading 'Non-magnetic'.

Magnetic	Non-magnetic
pins	
nails	buttons
paper clips	marbles
hair pins	toothpicks
staples	rubber bands
scissors	

Observation

The magnet picked up the pins, nails, paper clips, hair pins, staples and scissors.

The magnet did not pick up the buttons, marbles, toothpicks or rubber bands.

Conclusion

A magnet attracts magnetic objects.

Most magnetic objects are made of iron or steel.